Backtrack

BN Oakman

Interactive Press
an imprint of IP (Interactive Publications Pty Ltd)
Treetop Studio • 9 Kuhler Court
Carindale, Queensland, Australia 4152
sales@ipoz.biz
http://ipoz.biz/

Printed in 12 pt Adobe Caslon Pro on 14 pt Minion Pro Semi-bold.

ISBN: 978192830432 (PB); 978192830449 (eBk)

A catalogue record for this
book is available from the
National Library of Australia

Interactive Press

Backtrack

BN Oakman was formerly an academic economist. He started writing poetry in 2006. His poems have been published in *The Age, The Australian, The Canberra Times, Meanjin, Quadrant, Island, Antipodes* (USA), *Going Down Swinging, Mascara, Cordite, Tincture Journal, TEXT, Australian Poetry Journal, Eureka Street, Social Alternatives, LiNQ, Acumen* (UK), *Poetry Monash, Post-Colonial Text, Famous Reporter, Arena Magazine, Dissent, Burningword Literary Journal* (USA), *The Warwick Review* (UK), *Shot Glass Journal* (USA), *Best Australian Poems* 2014 and 2015 and elsewhere.

Bruce has published two full length collections, *In Defence of Hawaiian Shirts* (IP, 2010) and *Second Thoughts* (IP, 2014) plus two chapbooks with Mark Time Books. In 2016 the distinguished Australian actor John Flaus recorded 25 of his poems for a CD titled *What did I know? Backtrack* is his third full-length collection.

He was a recipient of a grant from the Literature Board of the Australia Council. *Second Thoughts* was best IP poetry book of 2014. He was a Pushcart Prize (USA) nominee for 2015. He reads from his work at poetry festivals, writers' gatherings and by invitation.

Bruce wrote short fiction for several years before turning to poetry. All his stories were published, most were awarded prizes.

He lives in Central Victoria Australia with his partner, Barbara Coish.

www.bnoakmanpoet.weebly.com

Interactive Press
Brisbane

Photo credit: Mary Leunig

for Barbara, always

Acknowledgements

Book design: David P Reiter

Almost all of the poems in this collection have been published, sometimes in slightly altered form, in journals, magazines or newspapers, specifically: *Acumen: A Literary Journal* (UK), *Arena Magazine, Australian Poetry Journal, Best Australian Poems 2015, Burningword Literary Journal* (USA), *The Canberra Times, Cordite Poetry Review, Eureka Street, Going Down Swinging, Poetry Monash, Postcolonial Text, Shot Glass Journal* (USA), *Social Alternatives, TEXT: Journal of Writing and Writing Courses* and *Tincture Journal.*

I am grateful to the poetry editors who have published my work, particularly those who have done so numerous times: Valerie Krips of *Arena Magazine*, Philip Harvey of *Eureka Street* and Mary-Jane Grandinetti of *Shot Glass Journal.*

My thanks go to those who have aided, encouraged, commented, criticised and enabled: Ross Donlon, Ross Gillett and Julie Phillips, Ian Irvine, Ian Britain, Leigh Mellberg, Jan Thomas and Charles Smith. I am indebted to Charles, who died during 2022, for his detailed, sensitive, and occasionally provocative, comments on my poems. Thanks are also due to the team at IP, especially Dr David Reiter and Cherie Reiter.

Others, through abiding friendship, have provided foundational support: Penny Oakman and Steve Brown, David Owens, Jane Gilchrist, Bruce and Sally Anne Clarke, Don Ross and Michele Swanborough, Dan Kerr, Graeme and Judy Baker, Carla Meurs and Ann-Marie Monda, Justin Moir, Dennis Carter and Karen Ward, Remon Eskandar, Marcia Saunders, Juan Carlos Jimenez, Sonia Velasco and Elena Garcia.

My partner, Barbara Coish, is always the first reader of my poetry and my debt to her is beyond calculation. Without her encouragement I would not have written a single poem. It is to her, with my gratitude, love and admiration, that this collection is dedicated.

Contents

Acknowledgements	vi
the island	1
Birthday	2
Sad Songs	3
Unfunded Empathy	4
expansive splendour	5
Il Gattino di Roma 1992	7
What to do with Trooper Ted?	8
Backtrack	9
divination	10
Lemons	11
Satisfactory	12
Remedies	13
Castaway	14
Questions for a Young Republican Militiaman	15
Like Stone	16
Requiem for a Revolutionary	17
An Inquisitor Composes a Sentence	18
sonnet for my Flybuys card	20
fragments	21
Sortition	22
agnostic prayer	24
Chicago '84	25
Yet why not say?	26
What to say?	27
The Day Before Australia Day	28
Avenida de America	29

One-Time Friend	30
Mm	31
Postcards from Dien Bien Phu	33
Dining with Goya in the Villa of the Deaf Man	34
he rang	35
Return	36
The Prison	37
the jungle	38
say it with flowers	39
no place like...	40
the ball	41
Sirtaki	43
A Valley in Spain	45
after	47
my father laboured	48
Lapping the Lake in the Time of Pestilence	49
At the Grave of Antonio Machado	50
your tiny hand	52
exegesis	53
shelter	54
Maratón	55
the day	56
Finisterre	57
Timepiece	58
La Reconciliación	59
ligna melanoma maligna	60
the circus	61
The Poet of Mycenae	62

the island

remember those burnished weeks?
how we talked of never leaving for fear
we'd corrupt the intricate alchemies of paradise
but when our time expired we flew south on cut-price wings
comforting each other with plans for a swift return
'when we've sorted a few things out'

we never returned to the island
snatched by duty's talons from the greasy runway
tethered by obligations without relent
burned by bitter frosts of compromise
long did we rail against our folly
like those fools who expelled themselves from Eden

yet, despite manacles of gainful drudgery
come-hither smiles from covetous death
the sky so low, the stars so often swathed in cloud
those gleaming days do not tarnish
blue-gold dawns, incarnadine sunsets, you,
and by early light if I reach for your hand

we dive into surf foaming on the lip of an ocean
listen for early stirrings of an onshore breeze
watch infinity's fires flaring in night's vast cupola
sleep under moonlight filtered through tent walls
and breakfast on mangoes stolen
from a ruined garden at the edge of a coral sea.

Birthday

after Ted Kooser's A Happy Birthday

I'll not set flame to wishful candles
nor boast of mere survival to my
peers but in that final fading hour
of the afternoon when crows shriek
at a setting sun and crickets chatter
evensongs I'll sit by a corner window
and scribble on a pad propped upon
my knee until night's benediction
steals across my page. Then I'll switch
on lights and observe the sustaining
rituals of evening before climbing the
stairs to sleep until a trio of magpies
nested in the garden warbles matins
at the dawn of another numbered year.

Sad Songs

in memory of Glenn Chapman

On Friday mornings he performs in an alleyway
by the supermarket, a hard-worn man who sings
sad songs with splintered voice and plays guitar
with such phrasing, dexterity and attack to hint

at green years shrivelled in quest of bright lights
that somehow never shone on him. Old velvet,
once crimson, now paler than unrequited love
and much nibbled by moths, lines his battered

guitar case. His smile when I drop a few coins
is a solitary brief blooming in a garden of dead
dreams, while notes flutter from strings pliant
to fingers' caress and skitter across the surface

of a fathomless sink of sorrows. I give money
in hope he'll go on singing sad songs, not only
for me but for every wounded nobody who in
silence keeps the stern and lonely vigils of grief.

Unfunded Empathy

On Monday, 29 July 2019 the prime minister of Australia declared he would not engage in 'unfunded empathy' by raising the Newstart payment which, at the time, was $277.85 per week.

an astonishing phrase from a believer
particularly an enthusiastic follower of the founder
who commanded us to love one another
even as he had loved us
it's more what you might hear from a Pharisee
or a friend of money lenders
those who made the temple a den of thieves
or perhaps it might be uttered
by an acolyte of the rich and powerful
a group as likely to pass heaven's gates
as a camel is to squeeze through a needle's eye
yet even such as these might shorten their paradisiacal odds
by dispersing their treasure amongst the poor
and let those hosannas in excelsis be fully funded
those hallelujahs in their thousands
be franked with the imputed dividends of love

expansive splendour

flesh tinged grey as if his core were shutting down
he boarded shuffling like his soles were smeared with glue
and died so discreetly a few hours shy of Abu Dhabi
he sat unnoticed until an attendant asked
what he didn't like about his untouched meal

a doctor (prised from economy, elevated to business)
felt for a pulse and shook his head
and I couldn't help thinking of Groucho Marx grabbing
a prone man's wrist and shouting
'either this man's dead or my watch has stopped'

then the cabin crew turned to mummery
eager to edit an unsettling final act
they fitted his body with oxygen mask and eyeshade
and made-believe he'd overslept
though fooling few as we filed away in Abu Dhabi

next day in the lounge of Madrid's Hotel Ritz
I reclined in expansive splendour
close by she who gives cause for me
to occasionally replace corks in bottles
and we drank to those who crave no lease on tomorrow

who know unkindly gods pour scorn upon our plans
that the dance always stumbles to an end
that the band packs up and slips into the night
that the dream rarely endures the rigours of the day
and then we drank to that grey stranger

who passed in high flight over the Indian Ocean
for him in his last ardent embrace
a winding sheet of opaque linen
to swaddle him from the egregious stares of the fearful
to him   and to the whole damn mess of it   *salud*   *salud*

Il Gattino di Roma 1992

returning from the Capitoline
I see a girl sitting on a swag
in the doorway of a shut shop
she's scrawled *Ho fame*
on cardboard ripped from a fruit box
she's stroking
a tortoiseshell kitten under its jaw
while it purrs and nuzzles her cheek
I think of my daughter
about same age and size
also brown hair and eyes
and similarly fond of cats
a child much loved
though too frequently from too far
a commonplace cruelty of divorce

I walk further along Via Cavour
almost to Termini station
before I pause
then turn to hurry back
to her doorway fumbling
in jacket pockets for banknotes
rushing with them protruding
between fingers of my clenched hand
as if desperate to place a bid
at guilt's grand auction
but when I arrive at the shop
she has gone
only the tortoiseshell kitten remains
to hiss at me when I stoop
to stroke her particoloured fur

What to do with Trooper Ted?

On Anzac Day I encountered a large toy bear tricked up
in military tunic Great War style, puttees, patches, slouch
hat, plume, rising sun badge – and named Trooper Ted.
Any child will take Trooper Ted to bed. Something jangles.
Jung's warning about sentimentality and brutality nags.
Is there something to be done? But what? Then I remember
Niki de Saint Phalle's creations from the 60s, the plaster
casts, her so-called shooting pieces. I rip off Trooper Ted's
plumed hat, trepan his exposed head with a breadknife,
scoop out polystyrene stuffing, shove a sealed plastic bag
of crimson paint into his chest cavity, stitch back his scalp,
replace his hat at a jaunty slant, stand him at attention
against a brick wall, aim my video camera and shoot him
several times with a borrowed rifle. Authenticity demands
a Mauser 1893, but I work within my means. I run images.
A body judders when a bullet rips through it, a black hole
smoulders where once shone an eye, a face shatters, an arm
floats in a pond with goldfish and lilies, a leg minus boot
and foot flops on a bed of forget-me-nots, guts spill into dirt,
incarnadine slobber oozes through coarse manufactured hair.

Backtrack

On a backtrack at Cardigan near Ballarat
after a July night's nadir plumbed minus 3,
they were found in a car *The Age* called
'home' for him (28), her (24) and a dog.

Butane from their heater is suspected –
tasteless, colourless, odourless, lethal
if leaking, a rival for oxygen if flaming;
lulling, drowsing, gentling unto oblivion.

In dew-damp grass lie cigarette packets,
fast food wrappers, a small syringe,
a scatter of budget bitter bottles, crushed
bourbon and coke cans, a teddy bear.

Such sordid manifests are rare for single
malt swillers and hundred buck snorters
who expire in private, swaddled behind
capital's opaque and dignifying walls.

Along one side of the track thistles thrive
amidst yellow gorse, the other is staked
and strained with barbed wire, the detritus
of brief passings strewn along the verge.

divination

pour your angst into those dark pools
eyes that rarely leave you while you talk and talk
about a life butchered into anguished anecdotes
you know she's listening, she nods
murmurs a few words, occasionally a question
much as she always has during your special hour
over weeks and months, sometimes years

and when, at last, she speaks at length
it's because she believes she's detected something
perhaps a theme artfully concealed in blather
something you think you want to know
or something you may never want to know
often a great crater in your soul you can never fill
no matter the scale of your smorgasbord of obsessions
money, work, booze, food, body, sex, order, dope
feel free to select your addictions
and try to remember how many times you uttered, 'why?'

someday you may begin to discern the skeleton of a narrative
blessed relief from all those warring anecdotes
and then, beyond talk, subterfuge and camouflage
you might seek, and find, solace in the realm of silence

no one promised a bouquet of roses flown from Vienna
only a vision of the austere majesty of truth
and, perhaps the greater gift
the opportunity to compose   your poem

Lemons

Any poem I write, never mind how brief,
seems always to need weeks to complete.
Recently I was tempted towards a belief
I'd finished a poem in less than five days.

Then I read of lemon trees soon to die,
how they bring forth crops so weighty
their limbs strain and splinter and split
and the earth around their trunks is soon
strewn thick with the rotting fruits of
such profligacy in the throes of death.

I looked once again at the poem and was
heartened to find several flaws hitherto
disregarded – nagging infelicities likely
to require some weeks of work to repair.

Satisfactory

is what he says when asked how he is,
knowing few will want to hear more
than *fine* or *very well.* And should he,
in turn, ask how they are, responses soar
to *terrific* or *fantastic* in tones tweaked
for triumph. Still, *satisfactory* seems
to disconcert, tendering neither gloom
nor enthusiasm, but apt for someone
of his age in fine health who dares not
sever the gossamer threads of formality
binding grief to isolation and stifling
tears, though not a sudden gasp that
bursts from the heart to merge unheard
with the clang and clamour of a moment.

.

Remedies

They belong to centuries smothered
in myth and mist, ruled by ritual
and attendant priests. A woman and

a man, deformed and unprepossessing,
were paraded along the pathways
of a settlement, he decked with dark

figs, she with white, all the while pelted,
cursed for every evil, damned for
every ailment, then dragged beyond

the gates, lashed to propitiatory stakes
and burned alive, purifying all
who dwelt within the walls' embrace.

When superstition evolved from
prophylaxis into blame, the *Pharmakoi*
were cursed no more and misfortune's

maledictions, cultivated in disregarded
darkness, were flung upon others:
dissenters, the different, disturbers

of stained silences, cranky prophets,
strangers importuning on the borders –
no garlands of figs and fire, instead

denigration and stigma, sometimes
bullets, blades and wire, always
a clang of iron clamping safe the heart.

Castaway

Not for me lists, those sentimental hits, easy tunes
from once upon my time. Just one canon, I want
the lot, secular or sacred, it matters not to a latter
day doubting Crusoe. My wind-up turntable will
broadcast cantatas, concertos, preludes and fugues,
the clavier so pleasingly tempered, that oratorio
for Christmas, a mass for occasional Sundays.
Before Easter come sundown I'll spin the Passion,
send exultation soaring on contrapuntal wings
to fly to my audience of indifferent stars, while
a lord of his wreckage, alone and forsaken, day's
catch on the fire, sand scoured for footprints,
keeps scanning dark waters for glints of salvation,
waiting, hoping – eager for the advent of Friday.

Questions for a Young Republican Militiaman

What to ask the young soldier who suspected
Antonio Machado was a priest in disguise and
arrested him in a cafe during the siege of Madrid?

Was it Machado's shabby black suit and crumpled
collar, or did his mellifluous voice seem honed
to intone heavenly reward for earthly servitude?

What did he feel when his captain, endowed
with superior education, told him his captive
was a *republicano ferviente* and a famous poet?

Weeks later, after the *fascistas* murdered Lorca
near Granada, did that officer tell him Machado
was now Spain's most famous living poet?

Did the young man, with humility's eloquence,
damn penury, serfdom and perfunctory schooling
and ask, 'Who, Comrade Captain, was Lorca?'

Like Stone

In Ballarat's Gallery hangs Davies'
Under the Burden and Heat of the Day,
a landscape drained dry, baked,
leached of colour. A stockrider
dismounts, offers water, comfort
to a distressed swagman. Davies
painted it after Gordon's 'Life is mostly
froth and bubble, / Two things stand
like stone, / Kindness in another's
trouble, / Courage in your own.'

Gordon was lauded by coarse colonials
deprived of refinement's smoothing.
Beyond poetry, not much went right.
At politics he was hopeless – couldn't
see much sense in it. With money
he was feckless, too poor to pay
the printer of his last collection.
In the saddle he was reckless,
and never the same since tossed
by Prince Rupert in the 'chase.

Friendless, fallen, indebted beyond
restitution's reach, he walked
into the scrub at Brighton
and shot himself. In his pockets
were several spare bullets,
as though he'd determined
not to make a mess of it.
He was thirty-six and alone.
Kindness and courage, with time's mercy,
are cold-chiselled in his stones.

Requiem for a Revolutionary

Che Guevara stares from the chest
of the young man seated opposite me on the train:
Alberto Korda's *Guerrillero Heroico* with beret, dark wavy locks,
cropped beard and a gaze disdainful of equivocation, eyes raised
scanning the parapets of Capital, probing for fatal weakness.

A man to love or hate – or both, darling
of student activists for over a decade, Castro's right-hand man,
lethally contemptuous of backsliders
and exploiters of the 'invisibles', as Neruda named
the numberless nonentities bonded in service to avarice.

In early days he was 'Ernesto', a trainee doctor sputtering
through Latin America with Granado on his old 500cc Norton
getting to know the emaciated faces of the *braceros*,
spending weeks working in a leprosarium, meeting peasants
deemed blessed if they possessed a single moth-eaten blanket.

Why does this young man display the visage of a revolutionary
50 years after his artful execution inside a hut at Vallegrande?
Shot creatively to simulate battle wounds, his half naked corpse,
lips split in posthumous grin, was posed for photographs
before a doctor hacked off his hands for fingerprinting.

The young man flips out his ear pods.
I catch his eye, ask why Che interests him. His features contort
as if accosted by a lunatic, a glare of quizzical resentment,
a fuddled, surly affect mocked by the composed conviction
of the face purchased with his shirt.

'Who the fuck is Che?' he says.

An Inquisitor Composes a Sentence

Sor Juana Ines de la Cruz (1648-1695) was a Mexican nun whose surviving poetry and other writings form part of Spanish literature's 'golden age'.

What is to be done with this opinionated nun,
this unceasing poeticiser who asserts, in defiance
of the teachings of the Apostolic Church,

that women enjoy a moral right to an education?
What to employ of the Holy Inquisitor's arts
of extraction, those intimate and intricately crafted

instruments for drawing from reluctant lips
admissions of heresies manifold and grievous
against Mother Church and the One True Faith?

How to calibrate the enticements to confession,
each with its own precise and delicate purpose?
Stripping is not for this woman, nor stretching,

nor compressing, nor the caress of steel or flame.
No, these are not fit for this loquacious agitator.
Sufficient to demand her signature be inscribed

in her life's blood on a declaration of penance
for having lived without religion in a religious
community. And as proof of sincere repentance

she shall divest herself of the entirety of her library
of books, of which it is rumoured there be thousands,
as well as her so-described 'instruments of science',

and all monies so garnered be distributed as alms
to the poor of the parish. But as God is Merciful,
Sor Juana may retain possession of any volumes,

should there indeed be such, as might nurture
and inspire her to devotional utterances which
from this day forth shall be the only poetry to

ascend from her lips to the Glory of Almighty,
Omniscient and Forbearing God, and in all else
by the Grace of our Lord, let there be Silence.

sonnet for my Flybuys card

driving home chuffed satisfied in a lazy kind of way
boot crammed with provisions enough for week
perhaps two settled no cash no credit just points
won absent-minded traipsing bank supermarket
servo suddenly a few hundred dollars less than
cleverly made prize for turning up not like tracking
the beast careful to stay downwind edge closer
closer rush hurl spear slices air squelch of tissue
smash of bone thrash crash writhe twitch light
dying in limpid pool of eye finish it blow from axe
home is the hunter joy children giggle glances from
women measured regard from men blood mingles
with sweat trickles between shoulder blades spear
axe bright with blood no place no pocket for plastic

fragments

winter

we walked
by the river
words limping across lips
the water's murk clouding your eyes
so grey

death of a friend

gone now
time's true witness
to those shared yesterdays
nurtured in memory of none
save mine

the aged poet

undimmed
his intellect
roams vagrant memory
searching for what he knows was there –
that line

an old photograph rediscovered

I scan
my eye's mirror
seeking the taker's face
someone loved beyond all my words
now lost

Sortition

Between May 1966 and February 1972, Australian men, after turning twenty, became eligible for conscription by lottery to serve in the Vietnam War.

I'd never met a Vietnamese, needed an atlas
to find the place, couldn't figure what we had
against them. But we were raised in the shadow
of returned men, the shimmer of lapelled
bronze, a presumption we in our turn would go
when ordered. Suddenly it was fortunate to be
too old or too young, to not find your birthday
plucked from the Tour of Duty Sortition,
a practice nurtured in Athenian democracy
reprised to coerce the unfranchised to arms.

My brother was called but ultimately rejected;
a shunning that broke no hearts. Ian studied
year after year, submitted his doctoral thesis
on the Monday after Whitlam won in '72. Lucky
John was too young – his mother insisted
every man's duty was to serve if summoned.
Kevin, a Chinese Australian, deferred until
he taught away the bond of his studentship.
A pupil in his fourth form maths class asked,
'How will they know you from a Slope, Sir?'

Most of us dodged gap years of sweat and khaki,
missing madness, maiming, napalm, agent orange,
learning how to kill and to piss ourselves out
of fear. Instead, we were granted head starts
with women, front marks in the greasy pole dash,
a less congested clamber to unremarkable lives.
How we quaffed the heady booze of freedom,

the privilege of stuffing up without military
intervention, never obliged to contrive answers
to questions we knew would never be asked.

agnostic prayer

He's not difficult to find. Black men stand out in rich
barrios. He'll be standing outside the supermarket,

smiling, a self-appointed doorman selling a magazine
nobody buys. I've known him for a few weeks in each

of several years. His name is Samuel. He's from Ghana.
His father is dead. He sends what money he can to

his mother. He has no papers and no work because
he has no papers. *Madrilenos* offer small change after

shopping. Passers-by sometimes approach with a euro
or two. Many dally to talk. He knows them, his clients,

various small and large details of their lives, what
to ask, friendly, without ever being thought a friend.

Before I fly home I hand him my leftover Euros and
he always asks god to bless me. I don't belabour him

with agnostic doubts for fear I'll debase his frangible
currency of gratitude. He gives me all he has to give.

I hand him a few crumbs swept from a table of plenty.

Chicago '84

Time edits memory. Maybe it was a block or two west
of the shabby end of Michigan Avenue. Cheap, clean,
convenient – all things my student guide claimed.
I've forgotten the name. A wit suggests The MLK Hotel
because I achieved instant, albeit brief, minority status.

I arrived in darkness. The desk clerk was young: sharp
suit, gold jewellery, rapid-fire speech. I asked where to eat.
'Go out front,' he said. 'Go left. Walk 300. You're outside
a diner. Don't turn right. I repeat: Do not turn right.'
I obeyed, ate, retraced my 300 steps, turned in, and slept.

By dawn's early light I ventured out – and looked right
into the maw of hell: incinerated cars, beheaded parking
meters, dogs scavenging in rotting refuse, riven
pavements aglitter with diamonds of smashed glass,
a man sprawled in a gutter, trousers about his ankles.

Some young men stared back at me. One gestured.
I retreated left. Later, when the fast-talking clerk was
at the desk, I thanked him for saving me from turning
right. 'Sir,' he said, as if humouring a child, 'who'll settle
your bill if you don't come back?' He did not smile.

Yet why not say?

after Robert Lowell's Epilogue

I want to say what happened,
commit memories, imaginings,
dreams, to words, and honour Lowell's
evocation of Vermeer's blue girl,
face burning with yearning, grasping
that precious letter, turning
towards the sun's stealing light.

I turn words to the light, watch
it shimmer over them, enhancing
brightness, shadow, the smooth,
the ragged, thoughts intended or
unintended despite my wilful desires,
then, in whatever is there I scavenge
and hope to find – a poem.

What to say?

Celebrants often ask the bereaved
to speak to a coffin
as if the dead might hear them still.
I've heard protestations,
excuses, wishes things
had been different,
the odd imprecation,
assorted verse, declarations
of unending remembering, never
accusation or condemnation.

And what might I say to you
when you no longer hear
my voice? Might I
intrude so much as a word
somehow withheld
over thirty years and not
proclaim my indolence, not
corrupt my tears with neglect,
not betray the perfect poem
of our silence?

The Day Before Australia Day

I dreamed I stirred from a dream, my
heart thumping, fearing the dawning day
to be your birthday, too late to post a card,
certain I'd failed to phone for months.

Then I woke and in that slow-to-clear fog
of returning consciousness remembered
you died years ago, no longer a need
to fumble to please, drear duty's debt

finally and forever discharged, no more
censures telegraphed via favoured emissaries,
the dream surrendering me to the day,
the sun coming up burning away the dark.

Avenida de America

back where I set out this morning I ascend from line six
the circle line with the deepest tunnels and hear, perhaps
feel, vibrations of a saraband bowed on a viola trembling

through the pulsating galleries of *Avenida de America* and
soon come upon an old man sitting close by an old woman
while he plays as once he may have played for audiences

who sat silent in vaulted halls and clapped when he paused
not storming homebound at the knell of a toiled-away day
but his cup is lined with grey velvet and brims with Euros

more than I've witnessed with busker or beggar anywhere
an approbation perhaps of Bach's meditations on mortality
which pursue me as I rise through subterranean arcades

fading to little more than distant sighs then dying before
I'm released into the Madrid night of crowds, clamour, cars,
sirens, whiffs of diesel, cigarette smoke, coffee, perfume

and I'm standing on a concrete island in *Avenida de America*
gazing at the veil of electric haze closing out the sky yet fired
with vain but eager hopes I might somehow glimpse some stars

One-Time Friend

Once upon a time we were related, emerging biographies
enmeshed, edited by in-laws, each complementing the other,
one brimming urbanity's assurance, one bashful and book
bound. Nothing much to fight over, neither wed to dogma
nor seared by acids of covetousness. After divorce sundered
those biographies we stayed friends – until he contracted
expedient amnesia, steeled his heart safe, scatheless, swore
fealty to inviolable pride while I blundered, lacking pole star
or compass, in outer darkness – and emerged changed. I never
claimed for the better. And yet I grieved when told he'd died.

Many were our good times. Pity the last 20 years or so.
He seemed a diffident revisionist, stroller of clean-swept
pavements, companion for flood-lit avenues, not a man for
the back streets where lesser cowards sometimes quaking go.

Mm

Marilyn Monroe, Bendigo Art Gallery, 5 March–10 July 2016.

So alive in death is how Juan Ramon Jimenez described
the poet Antonio Machado. We might say as much
of Marilyn though it's not her words that inform the
imaginings of admirers fifty years postmortem. A giant
plaster statue in Rosalind Park models her scene in *The
Seven Year Itch*, pleated white dress billowing in updraft
from subway exhibiting legs and underwear while she
blazes that ain't-this-wonderful grin. An image DiMaggio
hated so violently, demeaning for any woman of his, far too
much whore and no madonna whatsoever. Today they're
shooting selfies between her legs. She's also strung from
light poles in View Street wearing a gold lamé halter neck
gown plunging to her navel, her head tilted back just a
little, her hands behind her back, eyelids ultra-lashed,
heavily mascaraed, lowered so you can barely see her eyes.
Her lips scarcely part in an I-could-be-so-good-for-you
smile. Somebody said when she entered a room with
Miller every woman hated her – and every man hated him.
With gratuitous nastiness to both the press labelled them
the egghead and the hourglass. Hers is a made-up kind of
life. Neither blonde nor Marilyn nor Monroe. Mother in
and out of mental hospitals. Foster care for Norma Jeane.
Abused. Believed Clark Gable to be her father for most
of her life. Relationships tricky. Three divorces. Got
mixed up with Sinatra, the Kennedys and assorted
trouble. Difficult on the set. Late, moody and unlearned
of lines. According to Wilder an endless puzzle without
any solution. Years later, Clive James sneered 'She was as
good at playing abstract confusion in the same way that
a midget is good at being short.' Method, psychiatry and

drugs accompanied her back and forth through the porous borders of reason. Dead at 36, alone, naked, drowned in barbiturates and swiftly passed into the hands of strangers. Monroe knew betrayal as giver and receiver. Strasberg never distributed the contents of the box of her belongings to people she liked, maybe unable to find an affective memory for friendship's obligations. His third wife flogged the contents for millions at Christies in '99. But this show is not about troubling details. Think a 'celebration' of a creation called Marilyn Monroe, an invention of the studio and Norma Jeane – who spoke of MM in the third person. You can inspect some of her belongings in the gallery, see her fingers' impressions in old makeup, take an excursion to genteel necrophilia, visit a reliquary of the woman the cruel cameras loved. A woman utterly fabulous on the screen, said Wilder. A woman alive in death as surely as Don Antonio, someone we're still making into whatever we want her to be, someone still turning millions for people she never knew.

Postcards from Dien Bien Phu

for Don Ross and Michele Swanborough, who sent them.

On May 7, 1954, French colonial rule in Vietnam collapsed after the French garrison defending its fortress at Dien Bien Phu surrendered to the Viet Minh.

'Historical Photos', grainy, fuzzy, black and white:
Uncle Ho of course; a youthful General Vo Nguyen Giap,
student of Sun Tzu's arts, nemesis of imperial armies;
smashed aircraft; corpses wearing French uniforms;
Viet Minh pedalling bicycles; General de Castries
and his staff standing bareheaded, sheepish in surrender,
one officer gripping his shooting-stick as if expecting
unfurnished captivity; there's Nixon, Eisenhower's VP
visiting Ninh Binh before the fortress fell, neat in shirt
and tie, grinning, 'bell-cheeked' (as Lowell might say)
sent to 'Nam to check bankrolled puppets and proxies;
near him there's a smiling man, perhaps an 'advisor',
buttoned-up in defiance of swelter in a dark DB suit.

Scribbled across the other side – *Wish you were here.*

Soon, broken boys wing home mad or zipped in bags,
napalm sears the promise of morning, Johnson
conspires to capture hearts and minds, conscription
raffles the manhood of the young. Bitter is defeat,
spurned is surrender for flight across the seas,
deafening the clatter of dominos, pliant the spines
of reluctant allies – those designated better dead than red.

Dining with Goya in the Villa of the Deaf Man

Francisco de Goya, Saturno Devorando a Uno de Sus Niños, 1819-1823,
Museo del Prado, Madrid.

I'm dining with Goya in *Quinta del Sordo*, a villa
by the Manzanares he bought from a deaf man.
He has no reason to change its name. Evening's

gloom invades the room. The *pinturas negras*
loom from fitful shadows cast by frugal flames
from a pair of candles. We eat *fabada* assailed

by visual screams – wretchedness, hopelessness,
loneliness, old age and death ungraced by puny
promises of salvation's solace. Angels of mercy

do not ply Goya's glowering firmaments. From
my chair I stare at two peasants clubbing each
other to pulp in a bog. If Goya glances up he'll

watch an ugly mad-eyed old Titan, who fears his
children will usurp his powers, rip the head from
his naked child with his teeth. I know the moral

of the myth: age is devouring youth until, one day,
a child evades the savage maw, grows to maturity
and returns boiling for retribution. I shout at Goya,

'Francisco, is this to be our fate?' (He won't reply
if I use titles or formalities.) I bellow my question
four or five times. Finally, he raises his left hand

palm exposed. His right grips a spoon dripping
fabada. 'You think I paint what I don't believe?'
he says. 'Which *barrio* of hell do you spring from?'

he rang

for Don Ross

a voice made for poetry
asking of you post-surgery
your whereabouts in the labyrinth of cures

I spoke of blind turns and errors
of kindness, though mainly your courage
he recalled his one big scare

and declared he'd not want to swap
we talked of our teams' disparate fortunes
his more uplifting than mine

he said he was determined to visit
when he was over the 'flu
and insisted I tell you he loves you

of course I promised I would
that's when he said he loves me too
and I hung up for fear I might sob

Return

I return a stranger to a place once my entire world.
The taxi cruises the top end, the well-drained end
where plane trees cast shadows at precise intervals,
footpaths are asphalted, gutters concreted, gardens
of brick bungalows subdued without mercy, their
paths hard and narrow and straight. I'm from the low
end of town, where drains drain to, where it's fibro
and weatherboard and footpaths of gravel, where
the creek ran red on slaughtering days. The top end
was never my part of town and the low stopped
being home after I left for university. No wonder it's
so foreign now. Not that trope about things seeming
smaller. It's more like I've returned to a movie set
that's outlasted the poor players who strutted here.

Was it me who walked these tidy streets, wondered
if anything stirred behind lacy curtains, lurked behind
nothing-ever-happens-in-here facades? I recognise a
house where a girlfriend lived, she they made queen
of their begonias, though she ascended after I fled the
realm. Could that be a tennis court where I played so
earnestly, so badly? Somewhere around here there's
a church hall where the young clubbed, loose-bound
by fraying yarns of easy-come easy-go religion. 'It
feels like the wrong place,' I mumble. 'I'm driving
you by the shortest possible route, sir,' snaps the
driver. Her expression is so sour I figure she might
enjoy sucking lemons. I don't explain. Minutes later
we pull up outside the hospital. 'Visiting,' she says,
not a question, merely a silence filler while I fumble
for my wallet. I tell her my father is dying and I've
returned to see him. 'That'll be 7 dollars, sir,' she says.

The Prison

Cárcel Porlier, Madrid, 1936-1944

Turistas ask 'Why all this talk of civil war? It's long over.
How can it matter now?' Yet its legacy smoulders in laws,
street signs, buildings, in who is wealthy and who is poor,

commonplace corruptions of trade and governance, in what's
said and not said, what's remembered and what's feigned
forgotten. After lunch in *Calle Maldonado* I walk a couple

of hundred metres to the old prison. No plaques, no signs,
though unmistakeable from faded photographs: rectangular,
four levels, brown bricks, austere, windows no longer barred,

hulking over an entire block. It's now a religious school of
a church that lauded a dictator's triumph, his *cruzada* in
defence of 'Christian civilisation' (never mind his Moroccan

mercenaries). With Madrid besieged *Republicanos* locked
fifth column *Francoistas* in here. Victorious rebels in turn
crammed it with those 'who do not think as we do'. In nearby

apartments ancients might recall comings and goings, how
nights trembled with trucks hauling the doomed to firing
squads. *Para Dios y España* shout the stones of 'martyred'

Nationalistas. Losers rot wordless, though often unquietly,
in unmarked graves. A Compact of Forgetting, democracy's
Faustian dowry, cossets those with most to hide and gags

the dishonoured dead. Back at my hotel I ask the reception
clerk if many know the religious school in the same street
was a prison. 'Can anybody tell the difference?' he says.

the jungle

for Dennis Spiro Livitsanis

high school was red brick, old style, pre-prefab
with a panelled assembly hall dignifying the upper floor
where senior students flirted with private study
while lounging on tattered leather near the stairwell

one day, no idea why, I walked to the banister and let fly
Tarzan's throbbing two note animal rallying cry
and heard the glorious acoustics of my lofty lair
bear it bouncing through the murmurous air

come lunchbreak everybody talked of how
a stick of chalk shattered in mid word
teachers forgot what they thought they had to say
how a sudden silence drowned in surging waves of mirth

the headmaster stormed from his study muttering of anarchy
the head prefect sitting alongside me disapproved
but couldn't stop laughing long enough to reprimand me
and nobody ratted

my gilded name (below Our University Graduates)
is fading on polished panels in that assembly hall
none is likely to remark upon it nor squander
a thought on who I am or who I might have been

but if I am to be to be remembered for anything at all
I want to be known as a young man
(and a much older one) who'd seize every chance
to go swinging through the jungle with Jane

say it with flowers

when that final curtain falls upon the meek
those supposed to inherit the earth but never do

let their resting plots be overrun
with an abundance of Good Intentions
entwined with gentling clumps of Indecisions
woven with tangles of Burgeoning Regrets
and adorned with bunches of self-sown Recriminations

and what flora might flourish upon tombs
of those who claimed they knew the way
and left us wrecked on shoals of their ambitions

surely vigorous thickets of Rampant Hubris
bounded by clusters of Creeping Contempts
with tossed bouquets of Odorous Arrogance
and to decorate their strident stones
some tortured weavings of Creeping Ego
throttling thriving garlands of Everlasting Conceits

no place like...

after John le Carré's The Pigeon Tunnel

high on a roof they hatch in coops
atop the Gentlemen's Sporting Club
to be caged and carried down to earth
to fly dank tunnels towards the light
to burst sun-blind above the bay
easy game for the eager barrels
of well-primed sporting chaps
who roar and shudder with rabid glee
when every torn and bloodied bird
drops maimed or lifeless to the sea

survivors whether winged or whole
bank and wheel in befuddled fear
and unknowing of any better place
flap home to the coops upon the roof
to quiver and peck a captor's seeds
until again they fly the tunnels to the sun
to briefly soar above a shining sea
before the sudden storms of lead
the primal baying for the kill
the thunderous ejaculations of the guns

the ball

for Ross Gillett, fellow member, Western Bulldogs FC

We took heart to hear
our fierce young onballer,
an extractor with quicksilver hands
and flying feet,
is studying
American literature.
You say you'd like to discuss Dickinson.
I favour WCW.
Sound choices both
if he reads on devices
(as the young undoubtedly will)
lines squeezed
toothpaste-like
down
LH margins,
line breaks
rhythm
meter
rhyme
protected
from
annihilation by
automatic
resizing,
a bedevilment awaiting Whitman with his long-line neo-
biblical iambics,
The runaway slave dismembered thus:

And gave him a room
that entered from my
own, and gave him so
me coarse clean
clothes,
And our resolute onballer
will not be bamboozled
by Williams' urgings
to *Say it, no ideas but in things*
for in his trade
it's known by all
what matters
is the ball itself,
never the idea of the ball.

Sirtaki

in memory of DSL

At university, when we shared a flat, he'd play
his LP of the soundtrack from *Zorba the Greek*.
We knew music and sound bites by heart.

The movie ends on the seashore of Crete. Zorba
teaches his buttoned-up English friend to dance,
a scene still bright in memory many years since.

I blundered through a sirtaki at his wedding.
Sober souls insist I stamped it into submission,
terrifying any who dared share my flailing floor.

Youth's parallel paths forked after marriages, his
for 53 years and a life of resolute linearity, mine
for 13 and a long game of snakes and ladders.

Suffering he bore in the style of his favourite sport
– Greco-Roman wrestling. I favoured the footwork
of a punch-drunk boxer too befuddled to keep out

of the ring. Thirty-five years of separation were
concertinaed when he appeared at my father's
funeral to remind me of an incontestable fact.

With a large hand gripping my shoulder he said:
'We will always be friends,' as if this was something
as tangible as a bar of gold. No shilly-shallying.

No merging of lives. No pissing in the other's pocket.
It's not everyone's idea of a friendship. Decades
of silence, reunion, thereafter occasional meetings,

cards at Christmas, rare phone calls or emails. And
now a fistful of leaves is ripped from my narrative.
My most trusted witness to once-upon-a-time is silent.

Yet his gift, impervious to the surly intrusion of death,
never leaves me – like the grip of his hand on my
shoulder – and I am left with but one regret. I didn't

need join him on the baked earth of his father's stone
village or the myth-soaked shores of the Aegean,
but sometime, anywhere, I wish I'd thought to ask,

'Teach me to dance, Dennis. Teach me to dance.'

A Valley in Spain

for Juan Carlos Jiménez

In 1937, during the Spanish Civil War, the Battle of Jarama was fought between the 6th and 27th of February. Insurgent Nationalist troops attempted to capture the Madrid-Valencia road and choke supplies to the elected Republican government whose forces were defending the capital. The battle was a shambles and the outcome a stalemate. The road remained in Republican hands until the Nationalist victory in 1939.

Late autumn. The Jarama is sluggish,
waters low, banks burnt brown. Boys
racing bicycles stir columns of dust.

The river flooded during the battle,
surging so wide, so deep, that two days
of eager slaughter were postponed.

I won't polish away 80 years of tarnish.
The brass cartridge still grips its bullet
just the way you found it while walking

your dogs. A misfire. No mistaking a
firing pin's dent in a detonater cap. No
flesh torn. No bones smashed. Still, I

imagine a rifleman suddenly defenceless,
fingers fumbling to jerk an impotent
projectile from his rifle's breech.

This valley is sown with old ammo,
not all of it spent. Devotees of a dead
despot besmirch belated stones carved

and plaqued for the Republic's dead.
Small finds, such as your gift, turn the
mind to the innominate dead of a war

without a peace treaty, where loyalists
to a traitor's banner lie crossed, blessed
and hallowed beneath their names.

In a visitors' book at the small museum
in the town of Morata de Tajuña is an
entry in the hand of a militiaman from

the Lincoln Brigade who returned to the
field in '86. Above his name he writes:
For Justice. For Freedom. For Democracy.

All hacked from the convulsing body
of Spain while high-minded proselytisers
of like ideals stood by and watched her die.

after

a friend who dwells in Nordic realms
says despair spikes when daffodils
first burst from thawing earth
and buds emerge on apple trees
as if such harbingers of new growth
auguring dark days are almost gone
unsettle souls long locked in gloom

fragile flowerings of courage daunted
hesitant buddings of hope ill-formed
we dread being trapped in pitiless light
traipsing trails unmapped to sunlit gardens

my father laboured

my father laboured in unskilled jobs for 51 years from age 14
he was paid modest wages
he slept away his evenings in a tired armchair
he slept away the afternoons of his holidays
he never complained
he was a reluctant writer
he was adept at mental arithmetic
he surpassed his economist son at mental arithmetic
he offered no advice on career or girlfriends or anything else
he knew little of universities
he neither encouraged nor discouraged my lingering in them
he never asked about subjects I studied or subsequently taught
he taught me by silent stoic example to avoid hard labour
never a day passes when I don't honor his wisdom

Lapping the Lake in the Time of Pestilence

Autumn 2020, Lake Weeroona, Bendigo, Victoria

Three kilometres of asphalted track surround the lake.
In early hours, if you go clockwise, a morning sun will
warm your back. Go anti clockwise and you'll squint

most of your way. About 80 people circle the lake today.
Only two need not squint. The slow mow down shufflers.
The not-so-slow press hard upon the slow. The quick

storm past anyone in front of them. They bunch close,
plague-friendly close. Tyranny of numbers forces the
pair who walk clockwise off the track onto the verge.

Gasping, sweating, heaving, the mob shoves and elbows
for spurious advantage, eager to hunt a vanished dawn,
frantic not to be overtaken by a runner they cannot see

but have learned to fear from reputation, an athlete
who glides with the long, lazy stride of the gifted,
a player who reserves their best for the finish line.

The aberrant couple stroll into the unfolding day, yet
a while before the sun descends, perhaps there'll be
other sunsets, more seasons for leaves to fall from these

oaks and elms and plane trees, many evenings to watch
the light drain from the day, until, none knows when,
comes a caress of the gentling blanket of enduring dark.

At the Grave of Antonio Machado

Wayfarer, there is no road,
the road is made by walking.
– Antonio Machado

The rain is gusting off the Mediterranean.
It's not stopped since I left Girona this morning.
The sea is choppy, muddy, waves foam-capped.

In my pocket are weekday railway timetables.
It's Saturday. My earnest plans, thwarted
by brief but inconvenient illness, are useless.

I'm venturing the coast road, the route travelled
by Machado in the winter of '39 when he fled
for his life from Franco's rampant *fascistas*.

The old customs post stands derelict, redundant
along with francs and pesetas in borderless Europe.
I proceed on happenstance and a flutter of Euros.

When I stand by Machado's grave in Collioure
the rain eases. The bandera of the Spanish republic,
renewed so many times, clings to his defiant stones.

Poems, letters, notes, weighted against wind
by smooth grey rocks, dissolve into pulp. A strew
of sodden roses obscures his mother's name.

Machado, aged beyond his years, spent his last day
shuffling the foreshore struggling for breath. On a
scrap of paper he scribbled, *This sun of childhood.*

The letterbox bolted to his headstone descends
into his earth. I deposit my futile plans.
From one who forgot the road is made by walking.

A Spanish politician labelled Machado a tardy
correspondent. Yet it is he who first writes to us.
What protocol of the pen demands a reply to a reply?

The sun of childhood hangs low above the water.
By dying light I must find my way to Spain.
The wind has swept my footprints from the sand.

your tiny hand

driving to Melbourne
passing ruins of a pub incinerated for a payout
stereo pumping *La Bohème*
opera's one-time hottest couple
Roberto Alagna and Angela Gheorghiu
not yet the cooling, falling apart, separation, divorce
now it's the pulsating aria and duet
'My name is Mimi, Your tiny hand is frozen'

hope has not died
Mimi hasn't started to cough blood
Alagna's letting rip for all he's worth
the soaring intoxication of new love
and when his tenor commands those stretched high notes
I can no longer hold back my tears
a sudden outpouring blurring the road
compelling me to pull onto the verge
overpowered by thoughts of first meeting you

the blind date
those early transcendent all-consuming months
thinking of nothing other than you
my desk buried beneath papers I no longer cared a damn for
but so soon the crush of conformity
the lacerations of assorted afflictions
the kindly savageries of life-saving surgeries
the better angels earthbound, wings besmirched in mire
and yet the fire of those blazing days never quite gutters
still occasionally and unexpectedly flaring
never mind the rolling storms of shit
splattering the blades of an ever-swirling fan

exegesis

when seasoned academics gather
to hold forth on this and that
it's easy for a mind to wander
to less contorted subject matters
to language merely mildly tortured
disinclined to subordinating clauses
and lacking nests of fine-split hairs

my head and heart fly to Madrid
to one of several favourite bars
and before I raise my third cognac
I'm jolted by a declaration
'the exit Jesus of this thesis is dreadful'
and I cry out from near though far
'when was it ever anything else?'

shelter

he is waiting when I arrive
to launch my new book
my longest lasting friend
eager to laud my good fortune

we tread softly in each other's lives
swap emails rarely
write in early December
or when someone familiar dies

he tells me we must meet
now and then to remind us
of the endurance of our bond
and the rigours of the journey

as if he knows grid references
to dependable sanctuaries
no matter how fractious the mob
how unforgiving the terrain

I think of a sturdy tree shielding
a corner of some stony field
a presence taken for granted
until one day it's no longer there

we honour no talk of that day
perhaps some time hence
when one is out in rough country
and shelter's got harder to find

Maratón

Maratón de Madrid, 27 April 2019

It's a small bar with standing room for ten,
elbow to elbow. The owner's name is Juan.
He is not a small man. Everyone except me
calls him Juanito. Today every side street
is barricaded against the *maratón*. Juan and I
know neither of us will ever run a marathon.
I say, 'Thinking of having a run today, Juan?'
He turns from a steaming espresso machine.
'Ah, cómo estás, Señor Boss.' He knows my
name but usually likes to invoke Springsteen.
'La vida es un maratón,' he says. 'What breed
of fool needs run two at the same time?'
His machine hisses a sizzling affirmation.

the day

I knew there must come a day
when for the last time
you would reach for my hand
while we waited
to cross a busy road

the day went unmarked
not known to be the final day
until it was buried under many days
when you no longer
reached for my hand

and when at last I realised
the day had come and gone
I was stricken by sudden certainty
that for the remainder of my days
I'd never be so trusted again

Finisterre

I'm standing at the end of the earth – where
the old world ends on the rim of the Atlantic
a few kilometres north of the Coast of Death
where Galicians kept watch for the long boats

of the dreaded Northmen. Farther south lies
the cape where *peregrinos,* cleansed of sin
(if not of sinfulness), came to stare at the sea
after tramping the Camino and, in ecstasies of

superstition, trembled at tales of ships sailing
into the maws of sea monsters or plummeting
to oblivion over the brink of the world. Until
Colon sailed west few hazarded body and soul

upon such voyages. Afterwards many walked
along this coast and deliberated if to take their
chances in the Americas, to join purveyors of
slavery, syphilis, rape, robbery and the savage

pieties of the one true faith. And now, standing
where so many have stood before, I think of
the riven republic the far side of the ocean,
Gettysburg's hallowed resolutions diluted to

sentimental slogans, once proud institutions
supine in service of the few, odorous weeds
of mendacity thriving, their seeds floating back
to the old world borne on trade winds of hate.

Timepiece

It is lying in a shoebox, a casket of cast-offs,
forget-me-nots for memories I'd rather forget.
The glass is scratched, steel case pitted, leather
strap brittle. It crumbles at my touch. Initials
engraved on the case are mine. It ticks loudly
while keeping close to time when wound twice
each day. My paternal grandmother gave it to
me on my twelfth birthday, the last time we saw
each other. My mother, cultivator of grievances,
nurturer of sleights, banished her from our home
and so erased a kind, elderly woman, generous
beyond the frugality of her means, from my life.
She died of complications during surgery when
I was twenty – still obedient to tyranny's edicts.

I wore it through school and university and into
teaching until I neglected it for watches that kept
silent while telling time and needed no winding.
Now, its insistent ticking thumps like a heartbeat
of mortality. A tiny second-hand devours every
vanishing minute just as it did, albeit unheeded,
when worn on the wrist of a young man who knew
little about love – and far too much about cruelty.

La Reconciliación

Few *extranjeros* eat here, although it's just a couple
of blocks from the hotel. A *menu del dia* is chalked
on a black board. Only Spanish is spoken. The owner
is Luis. He's small, talks fast and moves even faster.
'La cuenta, por favor,' I say as he dashes past our table.
He calls to the barman by the cash register, 'Ignacio,
la cuenta de los Americanos.' I stir my turgid Spanish.
'Non somos Americanos, Luis. Somos Australianos.'

Minutes later he rushes to our table bearing a bottle
of cognac and two glasses and says, 'Lo siento, mis
amigos Australianos.' He dips his head, certainly not
a bow, more a gesture of respect unstained by grovel,
and says, 'I have no wish to insult you.' I've never
heard him speak English. A Madrileño eating nearby
lifts a glass and shouts, 'Viva los Estados Unidos de
Australia.' Other diners laugh. Luis leaves the bottle.

ligna melanoma maligna

After the swift, sudden diagnosis,
while we sat trapped in the grip of
traffic, you told me you'd not wish
to live if I were to die. I said if I'd
endured so many treks through the
arid valleys of treatments, drunk so
deeply from the brackish springs
of cures, I too might feel as you.

Weeks later, after my reprieve, you
seemed surprised by my evident joy.
I could think of nothing to say. Days
passed until I knew to ask: 'What fool
would not glory in being alive if they
might remain with one such as you?'

the circus

the day the queen died a memory burst from the vaults of time

a sweltering night when the circus visits a country town
the crack of a tamer's whip goading a lion through hoops
until it jumps onto a stool and snarls at its tormenter
elephants lumbering in circles   trunks entwined with tails
a pretty girl with a ladder in her stocking twirling on a rope
later she somersaults on the broad back of a cantering pony
suddenly a voice over loudspeakers demands attention
our king has died in his sleep   long live our new queen
a silence is requested   a lion caged outside the tent roars
the anthem crackles   a few know to change a pronoun

disordered decades scud across my mind as I struggle to recall

when an Australian boy indoctrinated in the myths of majesty
started a slow and faltering conversion to fervent republicanism
certainly not before he resumed his seat at that circus
before a bugle blurted   before they sent out the clowns

The Poet of Mycenae

after Alice Oswald's Nobody, and in memory of Charles Smith

after Agamemnon sacrifices their daughter Iphigenia
to persuade fickle gods to grant fair winds for Troy
he fears Clytemnestra's wrath might turn on him
while she rules Mycenae during his adventuring
so, he pays a poet, somebody never named by Homer
and instructs him to spy upon her and send word to him
should he observe so much as a hint of adultery

the horizon barely closes over Agamemnon's flotilla
before his cousin Aegisthus seizes the unfortunate poet
rows him to a rocky outcrop where he dumps him to die
a feast for birds of prey that leaves nothing of him but bones

whereupon Clytemnestra welcomes Aegisthus as her lover

ten years pass before Agamemnon sails home to Mycenae
a conqueror high on opiates of omnipotence
a king everywhere greeted on bended knee
a man seemingly indifferent to the fate of his poor agent
from whom he has received no correspondence
to warn of lethal liaison between his queen and her lover
who conspire to flatter, deceive, and murder him

during thousands of nights camped outside Troy's walls

did Agamemnon never reflect on his wisdom in hiring
a minstrel unversed in the dark arts of a dangerous trade
someone penurious after decades of devotion to poetry
who might lunge gratefully for a dangled purse of silver
to only later ponder his shortcomings
while dying on forgotten rocks, a nonentity shuddering
with every shriek and swoop of circling seabirds